TOOLS FOR CAREGIVERS

- **F&P LEVEL:** B
- **WORD COUNT:** 25
- **CURRICULUM CONNECTIONS:** senses, smells

Skills to Teach

- **HIGH-FREQUENCY WORDS:** a, I, my, with
- **CONTENT WORDS:** bananas, campfire, cookies, flowers, nose, popcorn, smell, soap
- **PUNCTUATION:** exclamation point, periods
- **WORD STUDY:** compound words (*campfire, popcorn*); long /o/, spelled oa (*soap*); /oo/, spelled oo (*cookies*); /ow/, spelled ow (*flowers*)
- **TEXT TYPE:** information report

Before Reading Activities

- Read the title and give a simple statement of the main idea.
- Have students "walk" through the book and talk about what they see in the pictures.
- Introduce new vocabulary by having students predict the first letter and locate the word in the text.
- Discuss any unfamiliar concepts that are in the text.

After Reading Activities

The book showed items that have strong smells. What are your favorite smells? Can you name what items have or make those smells? Are there any smells you dislike? What are they, and why?

Tadpole Books are published by Jump!, 5357 Penn Avenue South, Minneapolis, MN 55419, www.jumplibrary.com

Copyright ©2023 Jump!. International copyright reserved in all countries. No part of this book may be reproduced in any form without written permission from the publisher.

Editor: Jenna Gleisner **Designer:** Emma Bersie

Photo Credits: Serhiy Kobyakov/Shutterstock, cover; Edjbartos/Dreamstime, 1; Svetlana Serebryakova/Shutterstock, 2tl, 6–7; Lucky Business/Shutterstock, 2tr, 12–13; AsiaVision/iStock, 2ml, 14–15; ValeryMinyaev/Shutterstock, 2mr, 4–5; Elena Elisseeva/Shutterstock, 2bl, 10–11; marieclaudelemay/iStock, 2br, 8–9; Gelpi/Shutterstock, 3; Nataliya Arzamasova/Shutterstock, 16tl; Hue Ta/Shutterstock, 16tr; Pornsawan Baipakdee/Shutterstock, 16bl; Photoongraphy/Shutterstock, 16br.

Library of Congress Cataloging-in-Publication Data
Names: Nilsen, Genevieve, author.
Title: Smell / by Genevieve Nilsen.
Description: Minneapolis, MN: Jump!, Inc., (2023)
Series: My senses | Includes index.
Audience: Ages 3–6
Identifiers: LCCN 2022011601 (print)
LCCN 2022011602 (ebook)
ISBN 9798885240925 (hardcover)
ISBN 9798885240932 (paperback)
ISBN 9798885240949 (ebook)
Subjects: LCSH: Smell—Juvenile literature.
Classification: LCC QP458 .N56 2023 (print) | LCC QP458 (ebook) | DDC 612.8/6—dc23/eng/20220321
LC record available at https://lccn.loc.gov/2022011601
LC ebook record available at https://lccn.loc.gov/2022011602

MY SENSES
SMELL

by Genevieve Nilsen

TABLE OF CONTENTS

Words to Know 2

Smell 3

Let's Review! 16

Index 16

WORDS TO KNOW

bananas

campfire

cookies

flowers

popcorn

soap

SMELL

nose

I smell with my nose.

I smell flowers.

I smell bananas.

I smell popcorn.

campfire

12

LET'S REVIEW!

We use our noses to smell. Look at the items below. Have you smelled any of them before? Which smell is your favorite?

INDEX

bananas 7
campfire 13
cookies 15
flowers 5

nose 3
popcorn 11
smell 3, 5, 7, 9, 11, 13, 15
soap 9